The Everyday Soup Cookboo
Slow Cooker Soup
Inspired by the Medite

C000132123

by **Vesela Tabakova**
Text copyright(c)2016 Vesela Tabakova

Table Of Contents

Slow Cooker Soups – Healthy Dinner Ideas Inspired by the Mediterranean Diet

We live in an age when everybody is constantly on the move and putting a home-cooked meal on the table during a busy weeknight is incredibly challenging. But no matter how hectic your day is, it is important that you take a moment and enjoy a good, hearty meal. Because while there may be more than one right way to eat, scientists agree on one thing – the more real, natural, unprocessed food you consume, the better.

While it may look and sound difficult to cook healthy food at home, after trying out some of my delicious slow cooker soups, you will soon realize you can produce a nutritious family favorite dinner in no time. All my Mediterranean diet inspired soup recipes are super easy to throw together in the slow cooker in the morning. You just have to fill it up, plug it in, and come home to one of these cozy, comforting Mediterranean soups that will warm your soul and nourish your body!

Weeknight dinner ideas are hard to come by. For me, preparing delicious slow cooker soups is the easiest stress-free way of cooking healthy, yet amazingly tasty food for the family. My Mediterranean soup recipes use simple ingredients that you probably already have in your freezer, refrigerator, and pantry. They do not require complicated cooking techniques and are simply the best solution for fast-paced families who want tasty and healthy meals. At the end of a busy day a steaming bowl of heartwarming soup is the perfect answer to the question 'What's for dinner?'

Mediterranean Chicken Soup

Serves 6-7

Ingredients:

about 2 lb chicken breasts

3-4 carrots, chopped

2 celery ribs, trimmed, halved, thinly sliced

1 red onion, chopped

1/3 cup rice

6 cups water

10 black olives, pitted and halved

1 bay leave

1/2 tsp salt

ground black pepper, to taste

lemon juice, to serve

fresh parsley or coriander, to serve

Directions:

Add all ingredients to the slow cooker and stir to combine. Cook on low for 6 to 8 hours, or until chicken is cooked and carrots and rice are tender.

Remove chicken from the slow cooker and let it cool slightly. Shred it and return it back to the soup. Serve soup with lemon juice and sprinkled with fresh parsley or coriander.

Bean, Chicken and Sausage Soup

Serves 4-5

Ingredients:

10.5 oz Italian sausage

2 bacon strips, diced

2 cups chicken, cooked and diced

1 can kidney beans, rinsed and drained

1 large onion, chopped

2 garlic cloves, crushed

4 cups water

1 can tomatoes, diced, undrained

1 bay leaf

1 tsp dried thyme

1 tsp summer savory

1/2 tsp dried basil

salt and pepper, to taste

Directions:

In a skillet, cook the sausage, onion and bacon over medium heat until the sausage is no longer pink. Drain off the fat. Add the garlic and cook for a minute more.

Add this mixture together with water, tomatoes and seasonings into the slow cooker. Cook on low for 6 hours. Add in the chicken and beans and cook for an hour more.

Moroccan Chicken and Butternut Squash Soup

Serves 5-6

Ingredients:

4 skinless, boneless chicken thighs, cut into bite-sized pieces

1 large onion, chopped

1 zucchini, quartered lengthwise and sliced into 1/2-inch pieces

3 cups peeled butternut squash, cut in 1/2-inch pieces

2 tbsp tomato paste diluted in 5 cups chicken broth

1/2 tsp ground cumin

1/4 tsp ground cinnamon

1 tsp paprika

1 tsp salt

4-5 basil leaves, chopped

1 tsp grated orange rind

Directions:

Stir vegetables and spices in the slow cooker. Pour the chicken broth over.

Cover and cook on low for 8-9 hours or until the chicken is cooked through and the squash is tender.

Slow Cooker French-style Farmhouse Chicken Soup

Serves 5-6

Ingredients:

4 skinless, boneless chicken thighs, cut into bite-sized pieces

1 leek, trimmed, halved, thinly sliced

1 celery rib, trimmed, halved, thinly sliced

2 carrots, chopped

1 fennel bulb, trimmed, diced

1 cup frozen peas

4 cups chicken broth

2 tbsp olive oil

1 tsp thyme

1 tsp salt

Directions:

Heat oil in a non-stick frying pan over medium-high heat. Add chicken and cook, turning, for 3-4 minutes or until browned all over. Transfer to slow cooker.

Add all other ingredients to the slow cooker. Pour the chicken broth over.

Cover and cook on low for 6-7 hours.

Chicken Vegetable Soup

Serves 6-7

Ingredients:

2 lb boneless chicken thighs, cut in bite sized pieces

1 small onion, chopped

1 celey rib, chopped

1/2 small parsnip, chopped

3 garlic cloves, chopped

1 carrot, chopped

1 red bell pepper, chopped

1 lb potatoes, peeled and cubed

5 cups chicken broth

1 tsp thyme

2 bay leaves

1 tsp salt

black pepper, to taste

1 tsp summer savory

Directions:

Season the chicken well with salt, ground black pepper and summer savory. Place it in a slow cooker with all remaining ingredients.

Cover and cook on low for 6-7 hours or on high for 4 hours.

Slow Cooker Chicken Noodle Soup

Serves 6-7

Ingredients:

2 lb boneless chicken thighs, cut in bite sized pieces

1 small onion, chopped

1 tomato, diced

1 red bell pepper, chopped

2-3 broccoli florets

4 cups chicken broth

2 cups wide egg noodles, uncooked

1 tsp garlic powder

1 tsp oregano

2 bay leaves

1 tsp salt

black pepper, to taste

Directions:

Season the chicken well with salt, black pepper garlic powder and oregano. Place it in a slow cooker with all remaining ingredients.

Cover and cook on low for 6-7 hours or on high for 4-5 hours.

Add noodles to slow cooker; cover and cook on low 20 minutes.

Easy Turkey Noodle Soup

Serves 6-7

Ingredients:

3 cups cooked leftover turkey, shredded or diced

1 small onion, chopped

2 carrots, sliced

5 cups chicken broth

8 ounces fettuccine noodles

1 tsp garlic powder

1 tsp oregano

2 bay leaves

1 tsp salt

black pepper, to taste

Directions:

Add the broth, turkey, carrots, onion, bay leaves, oregano, and pepper to the slow cooker.

Cover and cook on low for 8 hours or on high for 4-5 hours.

After the 8 hours are up, cook the noodles for about 10 minutes in boiling water on the stove top.

Add the drained noodles to the slow cooker with the soup, and continue to cook on high for about an 1 hour more.

Slow Cooker Chicken Broccoli Soup

Serves 6-7

Ingredients:

2 lb boneless chicken thighs, cut in bite sized pieces

1 small onion, chopped

1 fresh garlic clove

6-7 fresh or frozen broccoli florets

4 cups chicken broth

2 potatoes, peeled and cubed

3 tbsp olive oil

1 tsp garlic powder

1 tsp dried oregano

1 tsp salt

black pepper, to taste

12 oz cheddar cheese, to serve

Directions:

In a skillet, saute onion and garlic with olive oil until onion is translucent.

Season the chicken well with salt, black pepper, garlic powder and oregano. Place it in slow cooker with the onion mixture and all remaining ingredients.

Cover and cook on low for 8-10 hours or on high for 4-5 hours. Serve topped with cheddar cheese.

Slow Cooker Sausage, Spinach and Tomato Soup

Serves 4-5

Ingredients:

1 lb ground sweet Italian sausage

1 lb spinach, frozen

4 large carrots, chopped

1 can red beans

1 jar pasta sauce

1 small onion, finely cut

1-2 cloves garlic, crushed

1 carrot, chopped

3 cups vegetable broth

1 tbsp paprika

1 tsp dried mint

salt and black pepper, to taste

Directions:

Brown the sausage in a pan.

Add the sausage and all the other ingredients to the slow cooker and cook on low for 6-8 hours.

Slow Cooker Corn Chowder

Serves 4

Ingredients:

1 can whole kernel corn, undrained

1 small onion, finely chopped

2 potatoes, peeled and cubed

1 cup diced ham

1 celery stalk, chopped

3 cups vegetable broth

2 cups water

1 can evaporated milk

2-3 fresh coriander sprigs, to serve

Directions:

In a slow cooker, place the potatoes, onions, ham, celery, corn, salt and pepper to taste. Add vegetable broth.

Cook on low setting for 7-8 hours and then stir in the evaporated milk. Cook for 40 more minutes and serve topped with finely cut coriander leaves.

Italian Wedding Soup

Serves 4-5

Ingredients:

1 lb ground beef

1/3 cup breadcrumbs

1 egg, lightly beaten

1 onion, grated

2 carrots, chopped

1 small head escarole, trimmed and cut into 1/2-inch strips

1 cup baby spinach leaves

1 cup small pasta

3 cups chicken broth

2 cups water

2 tbsp Parmesan cheese, grated

2 tbsp fresh parsley, finely cut

3 tbsp olive oil

1 tsp dried oregano

1 tsp salt

1 tsp ground black pepper

Directions:

Combine ground beef, egg, onion, breadcrumbs, Parmesan cheese, parsley, 1/2 teaspoon of the salt and 1/2 teaspoon of the black pepper. Mix well with hands. Using a tablespoon, make walnut sized meatballs. Heat olive oil in a large skillet and brown meatballs in batches. Place aside on a plate.

Add broth, water, carrots, oregano, the remaining salt and pepper and the meatballs in a slow cooker. Cover and cook on low heat setting for about 8 hours.

Add in pasta, spinach and escarole and cook for an hour more.

Lentil and Beef Soup

Serves 5-6

Ingredients:

1 lb ground beef

1 cup dried brown or green lentils

2 carrots, chopped

1 onion, chopped

1 potato, cut into 1/2 inch cubes

4 garlic cloves, chopped

2 tomatoes, grated or pureed

3-4 cups water

1 tsp summer savory

1 tsp dried oregano

1 tsp paprika

2 tbsp olive oil

1 tsp salt

ground black pepper, to taste

Directions:

Heat olive oil in a skillet. Brown beef, breaking it up with a spoon. Add paprika and garlic and stir.

Combine all ingredients in crock pot. Cook on low for 11-12 hours or high for 6 hours.

Beef and Chickpea Soup

Serves 5-6

Ingredients:

2 slices bacon, chopped

1 cup ground beef

2 carrots, chopped

2 cloves garlic, finely chopped

1 large onion, chopped

1 celery rib, chopped

1 can tomatoes, chopped

3 cups beef broth

1 can chickpeas, drained

½ cup small pasta

1 bay leaf

1 tsp dried basil

1 tsp dried rosemary

1/4 tsp crushed chillies

Directions:

In a skillet, cook bacon and ground beef until well done, breaking up the beef as it cooks. Drain off the fat.

In a slow cooker, combine beef and bacon mixture, onion, carrots, celery, garlic, chillies, beef broth, tomatoes, and seasonings. Stir until all ingredients are combined.

Cover, cook on low heat for 8-10 hours or on high for 5-6 hours.

About 1 hour before soup is done, stir in the chickpeas and pasta.

Italian Meatball Soup

Serves 5-6

Ingredients:

1 lb ground beef

1 small onion, grated

½ cup breadcrumbs

3-4 basil leaves, finely chopped

1 egg, lightly beaten

1 onion, chopped

2 garlic cloves, crushed

1 zucchini, diced

½ cup green beans, trimmed, halved

2 cups tomato sauce

3 cups water

½ cup small pasta

2 tbsp olive oil

salt and black pepper, to taste

1/3 cup Parmesan cheese, grated, to serve

Directions:

Combine ground beef, grated onion, garlic, breadcrumbs, basil, and egg in a large bowl. Season with salt and pepper. Mix well with hands and roll tablespoonfuls of the mixture into balls.

Heat olive oil in a large skillet and brown meatballs in batches. Place aside on a plate.

Add water, tomato sauce, onion and the meatballs in a slow cooker. Cover and cook on low for 9 hours.

About 1 hour before soup is done, stir in the zucchini, green beans and pasta.

Serve sprinkled with Parmesan cheese.

Bulgarian Beef Soup

Serves 5-6

Ingredients:

1.5 lbs beef shin, cut into large pieces

4 cups of water

3 carrots, peeled and cut into 3 inch pieces

2 onions, peeled and quartered

3-4 medium potatoes, peeled and quartered

1 celery rib, chopped

2 bay leaves

2 tsp salt

1 tsp black pepper

a bunch of fresh parsley, chopped, to serve

lemon juice, to serve

Directions:

Combine beef, onion, celery and water in a slow cooker. Add bay leaves, salt and black pepper.

Cover and cook on low for at least 12 hours or on high for 6-7 hours.

About 1 hour before soup is done, stir in the carrots and potatoes.

Serve with lemon juice and sprinkled with parsley.

Lamb Soup

Serves 5-6

Ingredients:

2 lbs lean boneless lamb, cubed

1 onion, finely cut

1 carrot, chopped

10 spring onions, chopped

2 tomatoes, diced

1/3 cup short-grained rice, rinsed

4 cups hot water

2 tbsp olive oil

1/2 tsp paprika

1 tsp salt

black pepper, to taste

1 tbsp dry mint

1/2 cup parsley, finely cut

Directions:

In a skillet, heat olive oil and gently brown the lamb. Add the meat together with all other ingredients into the slow cooker.

Stir, cover and cook on low for at least 12 hours or on high for 6-7 hours.

Hearty Lamb and Vegetable Soup

Serves 6-7

Ingredients:

2 cups roasted lamb, shredded

3 cups chicken or vegetable broth

1 cup water

1 cup canned tomatoes, diced, undrained

1 onion, chopped

1 large carrot, chopped

1 small turnip, chopped

1 celery rib

salt and black pepper, to taste

Directions:

Combine all ingredients in the slow cooker.

Cover and cook on low for 6-7 hours or on high for 4 hours. Season with salt and black pepper to taste and serve.

Creamy Zucchini Soup

Serves 4

Ingredients:

1 onion, finely chopped

2 garlic cloves, crushed

4 cups vegetable broth

5 zucchinis, peeled, thinly sliced

1 big potato, chopped

1/4 cup fresh basil leaves

1 tsp sugar

½ cup yogurt, to serve

Parmesan cheese, to serve

Directions:

Heat oil in a skillet over medium heat and sauté the onion and garlic, stirring, for 2-3 minutes or until soft.

Add the onion mixture together with the vegetable broth, water, zucchinis, potato and a teaspoon of sugar to a slow cooker. Cook on low for 6 hours or on high for 3 1/2 to 4 hours.

Season with salt and pepper, to taste. If you don't have an immersion blender, you can transfer the soup to a blender (in batches) and puree until smooth. Serve with a dollop of yogurt and/or sprinkled with Parmesan cheese.

Slow Cooker Tuscan-style Soup

Serves 5-6

Ingredients:

1 lb potatoes, peeled and cubed

1 small onion, chopped

1 can mixed beans, drained

1 carrot, chopped

2 garlic cloves, chopped

4 cups chicken broth

1 cups chopped kale

3 tbsp olive oil

1 bay leaf

salt and pepper, to taste

Parmesan cheese, to serve

Directions:

Heat oil in a skillet over medium heat and sauté the onion, carrot and garlic, stirring, for 2-3 minutes or until soft.

Combine all ingredients except the kale into the slow cooker. Season with salt and pepper to taste.

Cook on high for 4 hours or low for 6-7 hours. Add in kale about 30 minutes before soup is finished cooking. Serve sprinkled with Parmesan cheese.

Broccoli, Zucchini and Blue Cheese Soup

Serves 4-5

Ingredients:

2 leeks, white part only, sliced

1 head broccoli, coarsely chopped

2 zucchinis, chopped

1 potato, chopped

4 cups vegetable broth

3.5 oz blue cheese, crumbled

1/3 cup light cream

Directions:

Add the leeks, carrots, broccoli, potato and zucchinis to the slow cooker. Pour the vegetable broth over all of the ingredients. Cook on low for 6 hours or on high for 3 1/2 to 4 hours.

Transfer the soup to a blender, add the blue cheese, and blend in batches until smooth. Pour the soup back into the slow cooker, add cream, and stir to combine. Season with salt and pepper to taste and cook on low for 10 minutes more.

Beetroot and Carrot Soup

Serves 6

Ingredients:

4 beets, washed and peeled

2 carrots, peeled, chopped

2 potatoes, peeled, chopped

1 medium onion, chopped

3 cups vegetable broth

1 cup water

2 tbsp olive oil

4 tbsp yogurt, to serve

a bunch or spring onions, cut, to serve

Directions:

Peel and chop the beets. Heat the olive oil in a saucepan over medium high heat and sauté the onion and carrot until tender. Add the sauteed onions and garlic, beets, potatoes, broth and water to the slow cooker. Cook on low for 6 hours or on high for 3 1/2 to 4 hours.

Blend the soup in batches until smooth. Return it to the slow cooker, season with salt and pepper and cook on low for 30 minutes. Serve topped with yogurt and sprinkled with spring onions.

Vegetarian Borscht

Serves 4-5

Ingredients:

4 beets, peeled, quartered

1 carrot, peeled, chopped

1 parsnip, peeled, cut into chunks

1 leek, white part only, sliced

1 onion, chopped

1/3 cup lemon juice

½ tsp nutmeg

3 bay leaves

4 cups vegetable broth

1 cup sour cream, to serve

3-4 tbsp finely chopped dill, to serve

Directions:

Place the beets, carrot, parsnip, leek, onion, lemon juice, spices and bay leaves in a slow cooker. Add in vegetable broth. Cover and cook on high for 4 hours.

Blend in batches and season well with salt and pepper. Return to the slow cooker and cook on low for 15 minutes. Serve topped with sour cream and dill.

Curried Parsnip Soup

Serves 4-5

Ingredients:

1.5 lb parsnips, peeled, chopped

2 onions, chopped

1 garlic clove

4 cups water

3 tbsp olive oil

1 tbs curry powder

½ cup heavy cream

salt, to taste

black pepper, to taste

Directions:

Heat the olive oil and sauté the onion and garlic together with the curry powder in a skilled. Add to the slow cooker together with the parsnips, water, salt and pepper, to taste.

Cover and cook on high for 4 hours. Blend in batches until smooth, return soup to slow cooker and stir in the cream. Cook on low for 10 minutes.

Pumpkin and Bell Pepper Soup

Serves 4

Ingredients:

1 medium leek, chopped

3 cups pumpkin, peeled, deseeded, cut into small cubes

½ red pepper, chopped

1 can tomatoes, undrained

3 cups vegetable broth

½ tsp ground cumin

salt and black pepper, to taste

Directions:

Combine all ingredients in crock pot. Season with salt and pepper and cook on low for 6 hours. Blend in batches and cook 15 minutes more.

Moroccan Pumpkin Soup

Serves 6

Ingredients:

1 leek, white part only, thinly sliced

3 cloves garlic, finely chopped

2 carrots, peeled, coarsely chopped

2 lb pumpkin, peeled, deseeded, diced

1/3 cup chickpeas

4 cups vegetable broth

5 tbsp olive oil

juice of ½ lemon

½ tsp ground ginger

½ tsp ground cinnamon

½ tsp ground cumin

salt and pepper, to taste

1/2 cup chopped parsley, to serve

Directions:

Heat olive oil in a skillet and gently sauté leek and garlic until soft. Add in cinnamon, ginger and cumin and stir.

Add this mixture to the slow cooker together with carrots, pumpkin and chickpeas. Add vegetable broth and salt and pepper.

Cover and cook on low 6 hours. Blend in batches and return to slow cooker. Cook for 10 minutes more. Serve topped with parsley

Spinach, Leek and Quinoa Soup

Serves 5-6

Ingredients:

½ cup uncooked quinoa, rinsed well

2 leeks halved lengthwise and sliced

1 onion, chopped

2 garlic cloves, chopped

1 tbsp olive oil

1 can of diced tomatoes, undrained

2 cups fresh spinach, chopped

3 cups vegetable broth

salt and pepper, to taste

Directions:

Heat a skillet over medium heat. Add olive oil and onion and sauté for 2 minutes. Add in leeks and cook for another 2-3 minutes, then add garlic and stir.

Add sautéed vegetables and all remaining ingredients except the spinach into the slow cooker. Season with salt and pepper to taste. Cook on high for 4 hours or low for 6-7 hours.

Add spinach about 30 minutes before soup is finished cooking.

Quinoa, White Bean, and Kale Soup

Serves 5-6

Ingredients:

½ cup uncooked quinoa, rinsed well

1 small onion, chopped

1 can diced tomatoes, undrained

2 cans cannellini beans, undrained

3 cups chopped kale

2 garlic cloves, chopped

4 cups vegetable broth

1 tsp paprika

1 tsp dried mint

salt and pepper, to taste

Directions:

Combine all ingredients except the kale into the slow cooker. Season with salt and pepper to taste.

Cook on high for 4 hours or low for 6-7 hours. Add in kale about 30 minutes before soup is finished cooking.

Vegetable Quinoa Soup

Serves 5-6

Ingredients:

½ cup uncooked quinoa, rinsed well

1 small onion, chopped

1 potato, peeled and diced

1 carrot, diced

1 red bell pepper, chopped

2 tomatoes, chopped

1 zucchini, peeled and diced

4 cups water

1 tsp dried oregano

3-4 tbsp olive oil

salt and black pepper, to taste

2 tbsp fresh lemon juice, to serve

Directions:

Heat the oil in a skillet and gently sauté the onions and carrot for 2-3 minutes, stirring every now and then.

Add sautéed vegetables and all remaining ingredients except the spinach into the slow cooker. Season with salt and pepper to taste. Cook on high for 4 hours or low for 6-7 hours. Add spinach about 30 minutes before soup is finished cooking. Serve with lemon juice.

Broccoli and Potato Soup

Serves 4-5

Ingredients:

2 lb broccoli, cut into florets

2 potatoes, peeled and chopped

1 large onion, chopped

3 garlic cloves, crushed

4 cups water

1 tbsp olive oil

¼ tsp ground nutmeg

slat and pepper, to taste

Directions:

Heat oil in a skillet over medium-high heat. Add in onion and garlic and sauté, stirring, for 3 minutes or until soft.

Add broccoli, potatoes, sauteed onion and garlic into the slow cooker. Add water, salt, pepper and nutmeg.

Cook on high for 4 hours or low for 6-7 hours. Blend in batches before serving.

Creamy Potato Soup

Serves 4-5

Ingredients:

4 medium potatoes, peeled and cubed

2 carrots, chopped

1 zucchini, chopped

1 celery rib, chopped

4 cups water

3 tbsp olive oil

1 cup whole milk

½ tsp dried rosemary

salt, to taste

black pepper, to taste

a bunch of fresh parsley for garnish, finely cut

Directions:

In a skillet, heat the olive oil over medium heat and sauté the onion and carrots for 2-3 minutes.

Add sautéed veggies and all remaining ingredients into the slow cooker. Cook on high for 4 hours or low for 6-7 hours then blend soup in a blender until smooth. Add a cup of warm milk and blend some more. Serve warm, seasoned with black pepper and parsley sprinkled over each serving.

Leek, Rice and Potato Soup

Serves 4-5

Ingredients:

1/3 cup rice

4 cups of water

2-3 potatoes, diced

2-3 leeks halved lengthwise and sliced

4 cups vegetable broth

3 tbsp olive oil

lemon juice, to serve

Directions:

Heat a skillet on medium heat. Add olive oil and sauté leeks for 2-3 minutes, stirring. Add sauteed leeks and all other ingredients into slow cooker.

Cook on high for 4 hours or low for 6-7 hours. Serve with lemon juice to taste.

Carrot and Chickpea Soup

Serves 4-5

Ingredients:

3-4 large carrots, chopped

1 leek, chopped

1 can chickpeas, undrained

4 cups vegetable broth

½ cup orange juice

2 tbsp olive oil

½ tsp cumin

½ tsp ginger

4-5 tbsp yogurt, to serve

Directions:

Heat olive oil in a skillet over medium heat. Add in the leek and carrots and sauté until soft.

Add this mixture together with orange juice, broth, chickpeas and spices into the slow cooker. Season with salt and pepper.

Cook on high for 4 hours or low for 6-7 hours. Blend until smooth, return to slow cooker, and cook for 10 minutes more. Top with yogurt and serve.

Spicy Carrot Soup

Serves 6-7

Ingredients:

10 carrots, peeled and chopped

2 medium onions, chopped

4-5 cups water

5 tbsp olive oil

2 cloves garlic, minced

1 big red chili pepper, finely chopped

salt and pepper, to taste

½ cup heavy cream

½ bunch, fresh coriander, finely cut, to serve

Directions:

Heat olive oil in a skillet over medium heat and gently sauté the onions, carrots, garlic and chili pepper until tender.

Add sauteed vegetables and 4-5 cups of water into the slow cooker. Season with salt to taste and cook on high for 4 hours or on low for 7 hours.

Blend in batches until smooth. Return to the slow cooker and stir in the cream. Serve with coriander sprinkled over each serving.

Lentil, Barley and Mushroom Soup

Serves 4-5

Ingredients*:*

2 medium leeks, trimmed, halved, sliced

10 white button mushrooms, sliced

3 garlic cloves, cut

2 bay leaves

2 cans tomatoes, chopped, undrained

3/4 cup red lentils

1/3 cup barley

5 cups water

1 tsp paprika

1 tsp savory

½ tsp cumin

Directions:

Combine all ingredients into slow cooker and season with salt and pepper to taste. Cover and cook on high for 4 hours or on low for 8 hours.

Mushroom Soup

Serves 4

Ingredients:

2 cups mushrooms, peeled and chopped

1 onion, chopped

2 cloves of garlic, crushed and chopped

1 tsp dried thyme

3 cups vegetable broth

salt and pepper, to taste

tbsp butter

Directions:

Melt butter in saucepan and add mushrooms. Saute lightly.

Place mushrooms, vegetable broth, onion garlic, thyme and salt and pepper into the slow cooker.

Cook on low for 6-10 hours or high for 2.5-3 hours. Blend, season and serve.

Mediterranean Chickpea Soup

Serves 5-6

Ingredients:

1 can chickpeas, drained

a bunch of spring onions, finely cut

2 cloves garlic, crushed

1 can tomatoes, diced

4 cups vegetable broth

1/2 medium cabbage, cored and cut into 8 wedges

3 tbsp olive oil

1 bay leaf

½ tsp rosemary

½ cup freshly grated Parmesan cheese

Directions:

In a skillet, gently sauté onion and garlic in olive oil. Add to the slow cooker together with broth, chickpeas, tomatoes, bay leaf and rosemary.

Cook on high setting for 4 hours. Nestle cabbage into the soup, cover and cook until it is tender, about 20 minutes on high. Serve sprinkled with Parmesan cheese.

French Vegetable Soup

Serves 4-5

Ingredients:

1 leek, thinly sliced

1 large zucchini, peeled and diced

1 cup green beans, halved

2 large potatoes, peeled and cut into large chunks

1 medium fennel bulb, trimmed, cored, and cut into large chunks

2 garlic cloves, cut

4 cups vegetable broth

black pepper, to taste

4 tbsp freshly grated Parmesan cheese

Directions:

Combine all ingredients in slow cooker. Season with salt and pepper to taste. Cook on low for 6-10 hours or high for 2.5-3 hours.

Serve warm sprinkled with Parmesan cheese.

Minted Pea Soup

Serves 4

Ingredients:

1 onion, finely chopped

1 carrot, chopped

2 garlic cloves, finely chopped

4 cups vegetable broth

1/3 cup mint leaves

2 lb green peas, frozen

3 tbsp olive oil

1/4 cup yogurt, to serve

small mint leaves, to serve

Directions:

Heat oil in a skillet over medium-high heat and sauté onion and garlic for 2-3 minutes or until soft.

Add to a slow cooker together with the vegetable broth, mint, carrot and peas. Season with salt to taste. Cover and cook on low for 6-10 hours or high for 2.5-3 hours.

Blend in batches, until smooth. Return soup to slow cooker and cook for 10 minutes on low. Serve topped with yogurt and mint leaves.

Brown Lentil Soup

Serves 8-9

Ingredients:

2 cups brown lentils

2 onions, chopped

5-6 cloves garlic, peeled

3 medium carrots, chopped

2-3 medium tomatoes, ripe

6 cups water

1 ½ tsp paprika

1 tsp summer savory

Directions:

Add all ingredients into slow cooker. Cover and cook on low for 8 hours or high for 4 hours. Season with salt to taste and serve.

Moroccan Lentil Soup

Serves 8-9

Ingredients:

1 cup red lentils

1/2 cup canned chickpeas, drained

2 onions, chopped

2 cloves garlic, minced

1 cup canned tomatoes, chopped

1/2 cup canned white beans, drained

3 carrots, diced

3 celery ribs, diced

6 cups water

1 tsp ginger, grated

1 tsp ground cardamom

Directions:

Add all ingredients into slow cooker. Cover and cook on low for 8 hours or high for 4 hours.

Season with salt to taste and puree half the soup in a food processor or blender. Return the pureed soup to the slow cooker, stir and serve.

Curried Lentil Soup

Serves 5-6

Ingredients:

1 cup dried lentils

1 large onion, finely cut

1 celery rib, chopped

1 large carrot, chopped

3 garlic cloves, chopped

1 can tomatoes, undrained

3 cups chicken broth

1 tbsp curry powder

1/2 tsp ground ginger

4 bacon slices, cooked and crumbled, to serve

Directions:

Combine all ingredients in slow cooker.

Cover and cook on low for 5-6 hours.

Blend soup to desired consistency, adding additional hot water to thin, if desired.

Serve topped with crumbled bacon.

Simple Black Bean Soup

Serves 5-6

Ingredients:

1 cup dried black beans

5 cups vegetable broth

1 large onion, chopped

1 red pepper, chopped

1 tsp sweet paprika

1 tbsp dried mint

2 bay leaves

1 serrano chile, finely chopped

1 tsp salt

4 tbsp fresh lime juice

1/2 cup chopped fresh cilantro

1 cup sour cream or yogurt, to serve

Directions:

Wash beans and soak them in enough water overnight.

In a slow cooker, combine the beans and all other ingredients except for the lime juice and cilantro. Cover and cook on low for 7-8 hours.

Add salt, lime juice and fresh cilantro.

Serve with a dollop of sour cream or yogurt.

Bean and Pasta Soup

Serves 6-7

Ingredients:

1 cup small pasta, cooked

1 cup canned white beans, rinsed and drained

2 medium carrots, cut

1 cup fresh spinach, torn

1 medium onion, chopped

1 celery rib, chopped

2 garlic cloves, crushed

3 cups water

1 cup canned tomatoes, diced and undrained

1 cup vegetable broth

½ tsp rosemary

½ tsp basil

salt and pepper, to taste

Directions:

Add all ingredients except pasta and spinach into slow cooker.

Cover and cook on low for 6-7 hours or high for 4 hours.

Add spinach and pasta about 30 minutes before soup is finished cooking.

Heartwarming Split Pea Soup

Serves 5-6

Ingredients:

1 lb dried green split peas, rinsed and drained

2 potatoes, peeled and diced

1 small onion, chopped

1 celery rib, chopped

1 carrot, chopped

2 garlic cloves, chopped

1 bay leaf

1 tsp black pepper

1/2 tsp salt

6 cups water

Grated feta cheese, to serve

Directions:

Combine all ingredients in slow cooker.

Cover and cook on low for 5-6 hours.

Discard bay leaf. Blend soup to desired consistency, adding additional hot water to thin, if desired.

Sprinkle grated feta cheese on top and serve with garlic or herb bread.

Minestrone

Serves 4-5

Ingredients:

¼ cabbage, chopped

2 carrots, chopped

1 celery rib, thinly sliced

1 small onion, chopped

2 garlic cloves, chopped

4 cups vegetable broth

1 cup canned tomatoes, diced, undrained

1 cup fresh spinach, torn

black pepper and salt, to taste

Directions:

Add all ingredients except spinach into slow cooker. Cover and cook on low for 6-7 hours or high for 4 hours.

Add spinach about 30 minutes before soup is finished cooking.

Slow Cooker Summer Garden Soup

Serves 4-5

Ingredients:

1 small onion, finely cut

2 carrots, chopped

1 zucchini, peeled and cubed

1 box frozen baby lima beans, thawed

1 celery rib, thinly sliced

2 garlic cloves, chopped

4 cups vegetable broth

1 can tomatoes, diced, undrained

1 medium yellow summer squash, cubed

1 cup uncooked small pasta

3-4 tbsp pesto

black pepper and salt, to taste

Directions:

Add all ingredients except zucchini, summer squash and pasta into slow cooker. Cover and cook on low for 6 hours or high for 4 hours.

Stir in pasta, zucchini and yellow squash. Cover; cook 1 hour longer or until vegetables are tender. Top individual servings with pesto.

Crock Pot Tomato Basil Soup

Serves: 5-6

Ingredients:

4 cups chopped fresh tomatoes or 27 oz can tomatoes

1/3 cup rice

3 cups water

1 large onion, diced

4 garlic cloves, minced

3 tbsp olive oil

1 tsp salt

1 tbsp dried basil

1 tbsp paprika

1 tsp sugar

½ bunch fresh parsley, to serve

Directions:

In a skillet, sauté onion and garlic for 2-3 minutes. When onions have softened, add them together with all other ingredients to the crock pot.

Cook on low for 5-7 hours, or on high for 3 1/2. Blend with an immersion blender and serve topped with fresh parsley.

Cheesy Cauliflower Soup

Serves 4-5

Ingredients:

1 large onion, finely cut

1 medium head cauliflower, chopped

2-3 garlic cloves, minced

4 cups vegetable broth

1 cup whole cream

1 cup cheddar cheese, grated

salt, to taste

fresh ground black pepper, to taste

Directions:

Put cauliflower, onion, garlic and vegetable broth in crock pot. Cover and cook on low for 4-6 hours. Blend in a blender.

Return to crockpot and blend in cream and cheese. Season with salt and pepper and stir to mix.

Creamy Artichoke Soup

Serves 4

Ingredients:

1 can artichoke hearts, drained

3 potatoes, peeled and cut into ½-inch pieces

1 small onion, finely cut

2 cloves garlic, crushed

3 cups vegetable broth

2 tbsp lemon juice

1 cup heavy cream

black pepper, to taste

Directions:

Combine the potatoes, onion, artichoke hearts, broth, lemon juice and black pepper in the slow cooker.

Cover and cook on low for 8-10 hours or on high for 4-5 hours or until the potatoes are tender.

Blend the soup in batches and return it to the slow cooker. Add the cream and continue to cook until heated 5-10 minutes more. Garnish with a swirl of cream or a sliver of artichoke.

Tomato Artichoke Soup

Serves 4

Ingredients:

1 can artichoke hearts, drained

1 can diced tomatoes, undrained

3 cups vegetable broth

1 small onion, chopped

2 cloves garlic, crushed

1 tbsp pesto

black pepper, to taste

Directions:

Combine all ingredients in the slow cooker.

Cover and cook on low for 8-10 hours or on high for 4-5 hours.

Blend the soup in batches and return it to the slow cooker. Season with salt and pepper to taste and serve.

FREE BONUS RECIPES: 20 Superfood Paleo and Vegan Smoothies for Vibrant Health and Easy Weight Loss

Winter Greens Smoothie

Serves: 2

Prep time: 5 min

Ingredients:

2 broccoli florets, frozen

1½ cup coconut water

½ banana

½ cup pineapple

1 cup fresh spinach

2 kale leaves

Directions:

Combine ingredients in blender and blend until smooth. Enjoy!

Delicious Kale Smoothie

Serves: 2

Prep time: 5 min

Ingredients:

2-3 ice cubes

1½ cup apple juice

3-4 kale leaves

1 apple, cut

1 cup strawberries

½ tsp cloves

Directions:

Combine ingredients in blender and purée until smooth.

Cherry Smoothie

Serves: 2

Prep time: 5 min

Ingredients:

2-3 ice cubes

1½ cup almond or coconut milk

1½ cup pitted and frozen cherries

½ avocado

1 tsp cinnamon

1 tsp chia seeds

Directions :

Combine all ingredients into a blender and process until smooth. Enjoy!

Banana and Coconut Smoothie

Serves: 2

Prep time: 5 min

Ingredients:

1 frozen banana, chopped

1½ cup coconut water

2-3 small broccoli florets

1 tbsp coconut butter

Directions :

Add all ingredients into a blender and blend until the smoothie turns into an even and smooth consistency. Enjoy!

Avocado and Pineapple Smoothie

Serves: 2

Prep time: 5 min

Ingredients:

3-4 ice cubes

1½ cup coconut water

½ avocado

2 cups diced pineapple

Directions:

Combine all ingredients in a blender, and blend until smooth. Enjoy!

Carrot and Mango Smoothie

Serves: 2

Prep time: 5 min

Ingredients:

1 cup frozen mango chunks

1 cup carrot juice

½ cup orange juice

1 carrot, chopped

1 tsp chia seeds

1 tsp grated ginger

Directions:

Combine all ingredients in a blender, and blend until smooth. Enjoy!

Strawberry and Coconut Smoothie

Serves: 2

Prep time: 5 min

Ingredients:

3-4 ice cubes

1½ cup coconut milk

2 cups fresh strawberries

1 tsp chia seeds

Directions:

Place all ingredients in a blender and purée until smooth. Enjoy!

Beautiful Skin Smoothie

Serves: 2

Prep time: 5 min

Ingredients:

1 cup frozen strawberries

1½ cup green tea

1 peach, chopped

½ avocado

5-6 raw almonds

1 tsp coconut oil

Directions:

Place all ingredients in a blender and purée until smooth. Enjoy!

Kiwi and Pear Smoothie

Serves: 2

Prep time: 5 min

Ingredients:

1 frozen banana, chopped

3 oranges, juiced

2 kiwi, peeled and halved

1 pear, chopped

1 tbsp coconut butter

Directions:

Juice oranges and combine all ingredients in a blender then blend until smooth. Enjoy!

Tropical Smoothie

Serves: 2

Prep time: 5 min

Ingredients:

2-3 ice cubes

1½ cup coconut water

½ avocado

1 mango, peeled, diced

1 cup pineapple, chopped

2-3 dates, pitted

Directions:

Place all ingredients in a blender and purée until smooth. Enjoy!

Melon Smoothie

Serves: 2

Prep time: 5 min

Ingredients:

1 frozen banana, chopped

1-2 frozen broccoli florets

1 cup coconut water

½ honeydew melon, cut in pieces

1 tsp chia seeds

Directions:

Combine all ingredients in a blender, and blend until smooth.

Healthy Skin Smoothie

Serves: 2

Prep time: 5 min

Ingredients:

1 cup frozen berries

1 cup almond milk

½ avocado

1 pear

1 tbsp ground pumpkin seeds

1 tsp vanilla extract

Directions :

Put all ingredients in a blender and blend until smooth. Enjoy!

Paleo Dessert Smoothie

Serves: 2

Prep time: 5 min

Ingredients:

1 frozen banana

1 cup coconut water

1 cup raspberries

2 apricots, chopped

1 tbsp almond butter

Directions:

Put all ingredients into blender. Blend until smooth. Enjoy!

Easy Superfood Smoothie

Serves: 2

Prep time: 5 min

Ingredients:

3-4 ice cubes

1½ cup green tea

1 pear, chopped

½ cup blueberries

½ cup blackberries

1 tbsp almond butter

Directions :

Place all ingredients in a blender and blend for until even. Enjoy!

Antioxidant Smoothie

Serves: 2

Prep time: 5 min

Ingredients:

1 cup frozen raspberries

1½ cups orange juice

2 kiwi, peeled and halved

1 tsp chia seeds

1 tsp ground pumpkin seeds

Directions:

Blend all ingredients in a blender until smooth. Enjoy!

Coconut and Date Smoothie

Serves: 2

Prep time: 5 min

Ingredients:

1 frozen banana, chopped

1½ cup coconut milk

2 leaves kale

15 dates, pitted

Directions:

Combine all ingredients in a blender and blend until smooth. Enjoy!

Kiwi and Grapefruit Smoothie

Serves: 2

Prep time: 5 min

Ingredients:

3-4 ice cubes

1½ cup grapefruit juice

1 banana, chopped

2 kiwi, cut

1 tsp sunflower seeds

Directions:

Juice the grapefruit then combine with the ice, kiwi and banana. Add a teaspoon of sunflower seeds and blend until smooth. Enjoy!

Mango and Nectarine Smoothie

Serves: 2

Prep time: 5 min

Ingredients:

3-4 ice cubes

1 cup almond milk

1 mango, peeled, diced

3 nectarines, chopped

1 tbsp ground flaxseed

Directions:

Put all ingredients into blender. Blend until smooth. Enjoy!

Pineapple Smoothie

Serves: 2

Prep time: 5 min

Ingredients:

2-3 ice cubes

2-3 oranges, juiced

2 cups pineapple, chopped

1 carrot, chopped

1 tbsp ground pumpkin seeds

1 tsp grated ginger

Directions:

Juice the oranges then combine with ice, carrot and pineapple in a blender.

Add the pumpkin seeds ginger and blend until smooth. Enjoy!

Easy Vitamin Smoothie

Serves: 2

Prep time: 5 min

Ingredients:

2-3 ice cubes

2 pink grapefruits, juiced

½ avocado

1 carrot, chopped

1 cup strawberries

3-4 dates, pitted

Directions:

Juice the grapefruit then combine with ice and other ingredients. Blend until smooth. Enjoy!

About the Author

Vesela lives in Bulgaria with her family of six (including the Jack Russell Terrier). Her passion is going green in everyday life and she loves to prepare homemade cosmetic and beauty products for all her family and friends.

Vesela has been publishing her cookbooks for over a year now. If you want to see other healthy family recipes that she has published, together with some natural beauty books, you can check out her Author Page on Amazon.

Printed in Great Britain
by Amazon